Portfolio Take-Off

Stock Market Theory

Feliciano Bantilan

Text copyright © 2014 Feliciano Bantilan
All Rights Reserved
ISBN-13: 978-1501003172
ISBN-10: 1501003178

Limit of Liability/Disclaimer of Warranty:

While the author and the publisher have used their best efforts in preparing this book, they make no representations or warranties with respect to the accuracy or completeness of the contents of this book and specifically disclaim any implied warranties of merchantability or fitness for a particular purpose. The advice and strategies contained herein may not be suitable for your situation. You should consult with a professional where appropriate. Neither the author nor the publisher shall be liable for any loss of profit or any other commercial damages, including but not limited to special, incidental, consequential, or other damages.

Dedication

To the individual investor:

Invest a little time to understand the behavior of your portfolio return, like knowing that your portfolio is like an airplane. It needs a runway to taxi for about 15 years to take-off. Once airborne, it continues to soar skyward, to the sky is the limit, like the portfolio of Warren Buffett. If you do not aim your portfolio to take-off, then, you are missing the whole point of investing in stocks, in the first place.

Acknowledgment

I am deeply grateful to Jim Ryan for his valuable comments on the first draft of the book. They pushed me to clarify my positions.

Enrique Yaptenco deserves recognition for my photo on the back cover.

I express my sincere thanks to Kurt and to Hans for their critique of my arguments.

To Sr. Librada who unfailingly has been supportive of my writings, goes my abiding appreciation.

Reserving for last the most important, I am forever grateful to my wife, Cynthia, for her love and support. She has been an anchor in my life. To her go my eternal love and gratitude.

Table of Contents

Acknowledgment 5
Preface 7
Plan of Book 9
Prologue: Behaviour of Stock Markets 11
Introduction: Forces and Motions 14
Chapter 1: Stock Market Return and Current in a Wire 17
Chapter 2: Stock Market Return and Drunkard's Walk 21
Chapter 3: Two-Component Model of Stock Market Return 23
Chapter 4: Central Dogma of the Stock Market 38
Chapter 5: The Arrow and the Hoisting Crane 42
Chapter 6: Consequences of the Theory 48
    Attitude toward the Stock Market 48
    Investing Approach 51
    Managing a Portfolio for Take-off 56
    Parting Thoughts 59
Conclusion: What it means to Investors 62
Epilogue: Human Understanding 64
Appendix 65
    Axiomatic Presentation of the Theory 65
    Compound Growth 66
    Intentionality Lights up the Stock Market 69
About the Author 72
    Other books by the author 73

Preface

"It is a riddle wrapped in a mystery inside an enigma".
"Never, never, never give up".
Winston Churchill

The first quote expressed Winston Churchill's exasperation, on not knowing what action Russia would take. In the same vein, we are all exasperated in not understanding the behaviour of the stock market.

It was a riddle wrapped in a mystery inside an enigma. It was thus, it seemed to us, when we started to get interested in the stock market. We suspected the same feeling of so many others as well.

We kept at it; we kept at it; we kept at it…

Until, we pried open the riddle, unwrapped the mystery, and laid bare the enigma. Hence, the title of this book is "Portfolio Take-off: Stock Market Theory".

The claim may shock you. It seems outrageous for anyone to claim even "a" theory of the stock market.

Just like the theories in biology, the theory of the stock market we are proposing is not a quantitative theory. We are so enamoured of mathematics, of a quantitative approach, it blindsides us from *seeing what is there to see.*

We believe qualitative thinking, compared to a quantitative one, cast a wider net and thus catch what the other misses. We make a case for understanding the stock market. We claim we can understand a great deal about the behaviour of the stock market, in fact all its behaviours that really matter – without mathematics – which will not be available if we insist on using mathematical equations. In addition, such understanding has real-world applications and use probably to the great majority of investors.

The book attests to this belief. Ideas mathematical, there are; but, equations, there are none. We attempt to use qualitative thinking to squeeze the last "drop" in understanding the behaviour of the stock market.

You be the judge!

Plan of Book

The Prologue opens the discussion, with an overall characterization of the stock market as revealed by the theory.

The Introduction describes the elements of the discourse – the objects, the forces, and the space in which the motions of the elements take place.

Chapter 1 and chapter 2 lay the foundation for the two-component model of stock market return, by comparing two physical analogues to its behaviour: a current flowing in a wire and a drunkard walking along a line.

Chapter 3 builds the two-component model of stock market return, on the foundation laid out in the previous two chapters. It answers the key question: is there a minimum time for holding our portfolio of stocks?

Chapter 4 dwells on the implications of our ability to deduce the existence of portfolio take-off to unlimited growth.

Chapter 5 brings all the elements of our theory into focus with the metaphor: **the arrow and the hoisting crane.**

Chapter 6 details the consequences flowing from the theory.

The Conclusion ends with a remark on what the theory means to individual investors.

The Epilogue presents a reflection on the possibilities of human understanding.

Lastly, the Appendix contains three supplemental topics. "Axiomatic Presentation of the Theory" enables us to see the whole at a glance. "Compound Growth" gives us a sense of what compounding can do in the fullness of time.

"Intentionality Lights up the Stock Market" makes us realize we are both the causality and the randomness, driving the returns.

Prologue: Behaviour of Stock Markets

Our desire to provision our future by growing our money prods us to invest in the stock market. Randomness and causality are the two forces driving its dynamics. Randomness gives rise to the probabilistic behaviour of portfolio returns, while causality generates their deterministic behaviour.

The play between randomness and causality, between probability and determinism should guide our investing approach, as well as the management of our portfolio.

The influence of randomness on returns wanes with time to insignificance, while that of causality waxes to dominance. These contrasting behaviours inevitably lead to the prediction of the existence of portfolio take-off. At some point in time, causality's contribution to the return starts to pull away from that of randomness, growing the return over time without limit.

Empirically, the take-off time is about 15 years. With the existence of a take-off point established, our theory identifies two stages in the lifetime of a portfolio: taxi-time on the runway for about 15 years and take-off to unlimited growth over time.

During taxi time, the effect of randomness on the return – its fluctuations – often misleads investors into actions harmful to their portfolios, possibly preventing take-off. Moreover, to make matters worse the effect of causality – which is always positive – on the return may not be easily discernible.

Fifteen years, indeed, is a very long time. Patience is the virtue most necessary for investors – a quality rare among them. Stock market gurus, the likes of Warren Buffett, in the manner of biblical prophets, have been preaching to take the long view.

From its deterministic behaviour, the stock market promises asymptotic certainty, conditional on a sufficient wait –

about 15 years. After such a long wait, why is it only asymptotic certainty? Why is it not outright certainty? The reason is that the past cannot predict future performance. The past can only guide our expectation on the range of reasonable possibilities – and never eliminate surprises.

From its probabilistic behaviour, the stock market implies the need for a deep awareness of the weaknesses of human nature – our inherited traits. Such traits inherited from our ancestors – as short-time horizon, aversion to loss, greed and fear, herd mentality, etc. – stand in our way to success in the stock market, i.e. to attaining portfolio take-off.

Of special relevance here, is our weakness in statistical reasoning. We are poor intuitive statisticians. Thus, we fail to see the fluctuations of our portfolio return as natural processes arising from randomness, thereby requiring no action. All investing mistakes come from this mistaken view.

Probability has significant influence on market returns within the taxi stage, a time window in which investing is equivalent to gambling if our time horizon falls within the window. At this critical taxi-time – preparation for take-off – we need all the restraint we can muster to ignore the statistical fluctuations of our return. As the window closes, probability fades into insignificance, while determinism rises into dominance. At this point, our portfolio takes-off to the zone of unlimited growth.

An investor who does not understand the big picture described above will not likely succeed in the stock market.

Our **portfolio take-off theory** yields an understanding of all stock markets, past, present and future. The theory's universal applicability rests on the very nature of the forces driving the stock market.

In the end, the universality of the ***portfolio take-off theory*** ultimately rests on the sameness of human nature throughout the ages and across geographies.

Introduction: Forces and Motions

Isaac Newton comes easily to mind when one encounters the notions of forces and motions. Our mind quickly settles in physical space and time or space-time, as the arena where these forces and motions occur.

However, in this book, we will be dealing with forces and motions of a completely different kind and in a different space too. We will be moving in the two-dimensional space, defined by the stock market return[1] as one coordinate – the vertical axis; and time as the other coordinate – the horizontal axis.

We will be chasing the motion of the stock market in the two-dimensional space of *return* and *time*. This, as we say in physics, is the statics.

What are the forces determining the dynamics? The forces driving the stock market – driving its return[2], tracing curves in the *return-time* space – are forces of an abstract kind defined below.

The relationship between the motion of the stock market and the forces driving it is too complicated, as to be susceptible to expressions in terms of differential equations.

With the idea of statics and dynamics set, we move on to more specifics. In the stock market, there are two basic forces: one, randomness – the random buy and sell transactions; and two, causality – the net-buy over the long term[3].

---

[1] "Return" refers to price appreciation plus dividends.
[2] Stock market return, portfolio return, market return, and return – all these terms we use interchangeably. What they have in common is the portfolio of stocks. For instance, the S&P 500 index consists of a portfolio of 500 stocks of US companies.
[3] The definition of net-buy is in chapter 1 and chapter 3.

We were inclined to include a third force - the compound growth effect – together with the other two; but, for reasons of simplicity, we decided otherwise. Nevertheless, it is important to have an intuitive feel of what compound growth means to have a fuller sense to how big our portfolio could become in the fullness of time. We will address this issue in the Appendix.

Thus, the elements of our discourse are the following: the stock market and its return – whose motion or behaviour we seek to understand; the stocks and their prices, the constituents of the stock market; and the forces driving the motion or behaviour of stock prices, and thus, the stock market return.

Maintaining a two-dimensional screen in our minds enables ease in following the discussion.

The Underlying Story

The underlying story of the stock market is that of Randomness versus Causality. Randomness has a bad name. It is almost synonymous with "destroyer". Causality, on the other hand, has a better reputation. What comes to mind is that of "building-up". We then pass judgement on it by what it builds.

Nature is the stage where Randomness and Causality engage their contentions. Despite our initial impressions, each plays a positive, as well as a negative role. Randomness, for instance, generates variation upon which Causality, then, fashions into a variety of objects. Causality may build what could be a destructive force that Randomness transforms into a benign occurrence.

Specifically, in the stock market, Randomness has a negative role overall. It distracts investors into actions that detract from their goal of growing their money. It lengthens portfolio take-off time – when a portfolio grows with time without limit. It plays to our weakness – our lack of intuitive understanding of random events. Indeed, we are poor intuitive statisticians. We suffer underperformance, by mistaking statistical fluctuations for reality. Randomness may "ground" underperforming portfolios forever, unable to take-off.

Causality, on the other hand, has a positive role. From the outset, it grows our money. In the absence of randomness, it shortens the take-off time of our portfolio. At any rate, by its own strength, it out-muscles randomness when its percentage cumulative return is large enough so that no negative returns in the future when added can pull it down to a value below 100%. From that point onward, our return soars skyward – to the sky-is-the-limit.

It is a familiar story, we all see around us. It is the same story, as the emergence of order, amidst disorder or randomness – like living organisms.

Seen in this light, growing our money in the stock market is no different from growing a tree in our orchard. In both, we are dealing with the same basic forces, with the same basic dynamics.

Chapter 1: Stock Market Return and Current in a Wire

Here, we take the first step in laying the foundation – a physical basis – for the two-component model of stock market return.

To get an intuitive feel of the elements of our discourse, we start our investigation on the stock market with an analogy. The return of a portfolio of stocks – like the S&P 500 index, or your portfolio of stocks – is like a current flowing in a wire. We know a current consists of electrons moving from one point in a wire to another[4]. A portfolio return, on the other hand, consists of prices of stocks moving from one price level to another.

The electrons of a current flowing in a wire execute random motions, forward-backward along essentially one dimension, due to heat. However, superposed on their random motions is a causal or "drift" motion, a velocity in one direction, due to the applied potential difference or applied force between two points in a wire.

Portfolio stock prices, on the other hand, execute random movements in price levels, up and down, due to the random buy and sell by tens of millions of investors throughout the world, at different times, in different amounts. However, superposed on their random movements is a causal or "drift" movement, an upward velocity in price as a whole, due to the net-buy by investors over the long term.

This net-buy comes from investors' anticipation of share-price appreciation over the long term, based on the expected continuing growth of the world economy; on the continuing

---

[4] Classical electrodynamics describes well electrons of a current flowing in a wire. The classical description is adequate for our purpose. The most accurate description is the quantum mechanical description.

demand for goods and services, spurring technology innovations, resulting in the creative destruction of companies – all these ultimately depend on the continued growth of the world population.

Let us examine the mechanics of how the net-buy or net-sell arises in detail. At any instant when the exchanges are open, the market consists of a series of graduated offers to buy. In other words, say, Amy has an outstanding offer to buy 1,000 shares at $50. Beth offers to buy 2,000 shares at $49.875.

On the other hand, a similar set of graduated offers to sell is also going on. Cathy offers to sell 1,500 shares at $50.50. Dorothy offers to sell 1,000 shares at $50.75. A sale only occurs when one side surrenders across this bid-ask spread, i.e. Amy agrees to buy 1,000 of Cathy's shares at $50.50. The other possibility is that a seller may surrender, instead, Cathy agreeing to sell 1,000 shares to Amy at $50.

When buyers collectively want large amounts of shares of a stock, they have to keep surrendering to successive layers of sellers up the curve. *The rise in price is a "net-buy".*

We note that the number of shares bought is always equal to the number of shares sold.

On the other hand, sellers who unload large numbers of shares move along the curve in the opposite direction; they have to keep surrendering to buyers down the curve. *The fall in price is a "net-sell".*

A net-buy may occur after a "surprise" positive earnings report. A net-sell may follow a bad news. The rise and fall of prices occur largely randomly. To get an idea of the relative strength of price-rise to price-fall – in terms of the magnitude of rise to fall – we examine the long history of the stock market. We find that two-thirds of the time the market is positive. Thus, in the long term, the price-rise is greater in magnitude than the price-fall.

In other words, the net-buy is greater in magnitude than the net-sell over a long period.

To look at the notion of net-buy in another way is to look at returns, whether of a single stock or a group of stocks in a portfolio: a positive return means a net-buy; similarly, a negative return, a net-sell. We will revisit this view in chapter 3.

What have we achieved so far? We have identified the two forces acting simultaneously making the stock market return undergo a composite motion.

Imagine a wiggly line starting at zero time and 100% return (our initial capital), tracing a path meandering up and down in the *return-time* space; but overall has a net upward movement along the return axis. We just gave a generic description of a plot of a stock market return.

Ultimately, as we learned in Economics 101, supply and demand determine stock prices, just like the price of any commodity. In the short term, the supply of shares of stocks is constant. The time horizon for the supply of new shares is long—in years. The creation of new shares by the process of an IPO, initial public offering, of a new company goes through many steps set by Government regulators. The time to complete the requirements is in years. In addition, share buybacks by companies and mergers of companies to reduce the number of shares take time in years. That is the supply side.

The demand side has both a short-time component and a long-time component. The psychological disposition of an investor at a given moment may prod her to buy or sell shares of company XYZ. Perhaps, the news on the housing market sways her to buy or sell. The short-time wiggles in stock prices arise from such purchases or sales. Other investors, on the other hand, who are conversant with the shifting tide in the supply side, may buy or sell stocks accordingly. Still other investors examine the overall outlook of the economy to inform their buy and sell of stock shares. Such purchases or sales from these investors shape the long-time component on the demand side.

Summary

In resume, the motion or behavior of stock market return is not all or completely random; nor is it purely causal or completely determinate. It is a composite motion: random and causal.

To see the forces in another light, the short-term sentiments of investors comprise the random forces, the long-term sentiments, the causal forces. Over the long term, the net-buy is greater in magnitude than the net-sell. Ultimately, supply and demand determine share prices.

By identifying the component parts of stock market return, with their corresponding forces, we now have a conceptual handle enabling us to separate out the contribution of each – randomness and causality. Our ability to separate the effects of the two forces enables us to predict an important quantity, a *universal property* of stock markets – portfolio take-off to unlimited growth, or, the minimum time for holding our investments in stocks. This quantity has direct implications on how we invest and how we manage our portfolio.

The next step is to see how these two forces play out in time. However, before we do that, let us have another way of looking at the behavior of stock market return.

Chapter 2: Stock Market Return and Drunkard's Walk

In this chapter, we strengthen the foundation of the two-component model of stock market return laid out in chapter 1.

It is beneficial to have more than one way of looking at something, the more so if that something is important. For, then, our mind will have more "hooks" to secure its understanding.

To get another view on the causal and the random forces at work in the stock market, driving its return, let us use another analogy to think about returns—a drunkard walking in one dimension.

The return of the stock market is like a drunkard walking along a line. At every step, a coin toss decides which direction he goes - heads, drunkard moves forward, and tails, backward. The step backward is constant in length; the step forward is longer and increases with time.

The situation described essentially models the stock market return. The backward step corresponds to a sell that sends the price down; the forward step, to a buy that sends the price up; the difference between forward and backward step, to the fact the net-buy is greater in magnitude than the net-sell over the long term; and the increasing length of the forward step, to the compound growth effect.

We let the drunkard walk for a long time. We find him after a long time to be at some distance from the origin in the forward direction. If we plot the distance from the origin along the y-axis, and the time along the x-axis, then we have a curve that moves up and down, but has an overall "drift" upward.

Thus, we get an intuitive sense of the component motions: the random part from the coin toss; and the causal part from the difference between backward and forward step, and the compounding effect from the forward step increasing in length with time.

Translating back to reality, the tens of millions of buy and sell transactions at different times in different amounts give rise to the random part; the net-buy over the long term coming from the anticipation of share-price appreciation based on trends of economic growth constitutes the causal part.

With the two analogies – a current flowing in a wire and a drunkard walking along a line – firmly set in our minds, we move on to build the two-component model of stock market return in detail.

Chapter 3: Two-Component Model of Stock Market Return

The Heart of the Theory

The two-component model of stock market return is the heart of the theory we are proposing. Our theory stands or falls with the model. The accuracy with which the model components correspond to stock market reality determines its usefulness.

An indicator of model accuracy is its predictions, together with their empirical verifications. Another is its explanatory power, say, for the approach and success of Warren Buffett, as well as the failures of others.

The Stock Market

The stock market, in its widest sense, refers to the worldwide community of institutions and individuals involved in the regulation, maintenance, purchase and sale of securities.

It may refer to country-specific communities dealing in stocks or securities, like the Tokyo stock market.

The sense of the stock market in this book is one like the meaning expressed in the following statement: "Last year, we topped the market by 6 points – we mean our portfolio of stocks returned 38%, against the 32% return of the S&P 500 index in 2013". The market referred here is the US stock market. The specific index used as a benchmark is the S&P 500 index.

There are many different indices to use as indicators of the US stock market. However, the general behaviour of all stock markets and of all indices is the same. *We are attempting to understand this general behaviour.*

Understanding the behaviour of the return of the S&P 500 index or the return of your portfolio – is to understand the behaviour of stock markets in general.

Understanding the Behaviour of the Stock Market

There are a few super-successful investors, like Warren Buffett. On the other hand, there are tens of millions of individual investors, who struggle with huge underperformance of their stock portfolios and who when a bear market comes invariably join the party – giving great discounts off their purchase price to the already very rich.

What is the difference between Warren Buffett and the tens of millions of individual investors? The BIG difference that makes ALL the difference is that Warren Buffett understands something that the tens of millions of individual investors do not: *the behaviour of the stock market.*

This book aims to establish a theory of the behaviour of stock market return (we suspect the same basic understanding as Warren Buffett's) and explain it to individual investors.

Portfolio Take-off Theory

What follows is our **portfolio take-off theory**. It directly results from the play of the two forces driving the dynamics of stock market returns: randomness and causality.

Randomness Drives Stock Market Returns

As we saw in the previous chapters, the buy and sell transactions by tens of millions of investors worldwide, at different times, in varying amounts, are the elements of the random force. They arise from the "heat status" of investors— "hot" or "cold" toward shares of stocks.

In principle, we can trace the impact of each purchase or sale on the return—in the same way we can in principle follow the impact of molecules in a gas on the walls of the container—in practice, we can only deal with the situation statistically.

Even granting that we know the details described above, does that knowledge avail us anything? It avails us nothing. All we get is noise.

Randomness gives rise to the statistical behavior of returns. That is why our return fluctuates. We experience emotional high and low, as we see alternating "green" and "red" numbers in our portfolio.

The fluctuation in the value of our return—positive and negative—is what we readily see and feel daily. It is the source of anxiety, as well as investing mistakes. It is the focus of our emotional response.

Causality Drives Stock Market Returns

On the other hand, as we also saw in chapter 1 and 2, the anticipations of share-price appreciation in the future based on investors' perception of the upward trend of the growth of the Economy, in particular the upward trend of the growth of the business of the company underlying the stock—are the elements of the causal force.

More investors are positive about the future and thus the magnitude of the net-buy is greater than the net-sell over the long term. This difference ultimately springs from our desire to provision our future by growing our money.

In the short term, this upward drift or trend is visually not obvious. This is especially true when our portfolio is down. Nevertheless, it is there, hidden among the numbers—both positive and negative. We can calculate the average growth rate over the period, the so-called CAGR[5] (compound annualized growth rate). We see the drift motion as real through our calculation of CAGR.

At this point, it is not clear, how we can separate the effects from the two driving forces. As we will show, time will untangle the entangled effects from randomness and causality.

Causality versus Randomness

How do the dynamics of each force behave over time? Do both grow in strength with time? Is there a point of stalemate, where the two lock horns in place? Will one eventually dominate the other?

As we will see, when randomness is at work, we let time do the disengaging for us. In the end, randomness drops into insignificance, leaving causality in dominance.

Dynamics at Different Time Scales

Here, we examine the pattern of behaviour of three quantities over time: randomness, causality, and probability of losing money. Our analysis of return data will show that as time increases, causality increases, while randomness, as well as the probability of losing money, decreases.

This implies there is a length of time when the deterministic behaviour of return grows to dominance, while the stochastic or probabilistic behaviour fades into insignificance. This is also the point in time when the probability of losing money asymptotically approaches zero.

---

[5] A way of computing CAGR, given, say, the yearly returns is the following: $[(1+R1)*(1+R2)*\ldots(1+Rn)]^{\wedge}(1/n) - 1$, where R1, R2, Rn are the yearly returns.

We will relate this length of time resulting from the analysis of return data to the time determined from the dynamics of the forces driving the stock market.

Let us consider specific possible scenarios. Let us look at, say, the period spanning from the Great Depression to the present, from 1928 to 2013 – 86 years. Say, we have data of yearly returns[6] of the US stock market as measured by the S&P 500 index[7]. With the data, we can calculate the return for any period shorter than 86 years.

In the following discussion, five Figures show plots of the S&P 500 net return for five different periods. You do not have to squint to decipher the labels – just ignore the labels. Focus your attention on the plots themselves; they are there to give a qualitative impression in support of the arguments.

With that note on how to view the Figures, we move on.

At different time scales, the return exhibits different behaviour. If we plot the 86 one-year returns (see Figure 1), we easily see both causality and randomness at work. Notice there are many more columns above the zero-return line and longer, compared to those below. This fact is an indication of a net-buy over the long term.

Definition of "net buy" over the Long Term

To enhance our discussion of net-buy in chapter 1, we now elaborate on another way of looking at it, via the returns. Figure 1 shows the 86 yearly returns of the S&P 500 index, from 1928 to 2013. Over the whole period of 86 years, it is obvious the price rise was greater than the price fall – as already noted, there are more columns above and longer than below the zero-

---

[6] Returns include dividends.
[7] Data source:
http://www.stern.nyu.edu/~adamodar/pc/datasets/histretSP.xls

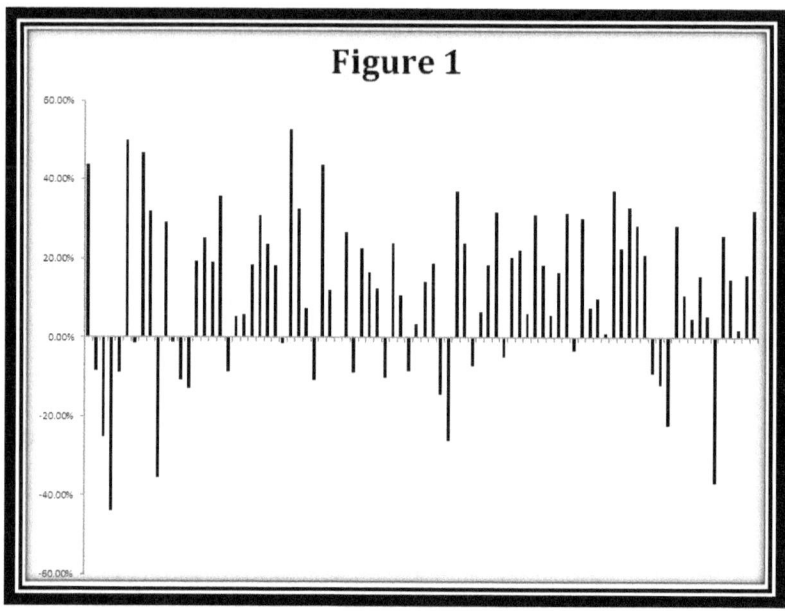

Figure 1

return line. The cumulative return must be positive for the whole period; it was 255,553.3%. We say there was a "net buy" over the 86-year period.

Periods shorter than 86 years had also a "net buy". The one-year period in 1928 had a net-buy; the cumulative return was 143.8%. The two-year period, 1928 to 1929, had a net buy: the cumulative return was 131.9%. The 8-year period, from 1928 to 1935, had a net buy, with a cumulative return of 110.2%. There are many more periods exhibiting a net-buy – a positive return. This is the concept of a net-buy – a positive return. Moreover, "over the long term" means the period in which the return is positive – ranging from a year, two years, or any number of years.

This concept of net-buy makes the contribution of the causal force to returns strictly positive. This is in contrast to the random force, whose contribution to returns can be positive, or,

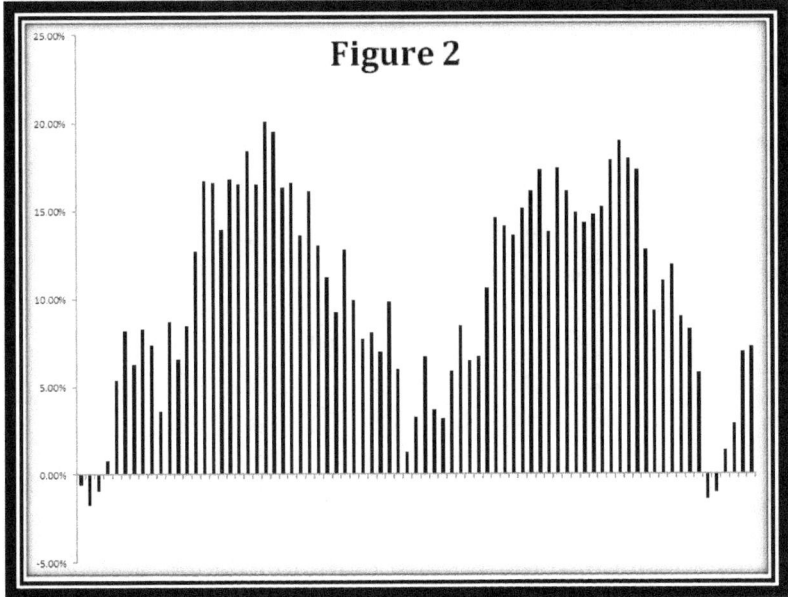

Figure 2

negative. This distinction will facilitate our proof of the existence of portfolio take-off in a later section.

Increasing Time Scales

For a one-year holding time (see Figure 1), the probability of losing money is 24/86 or 27.9%. [Note in calculating probabilities, we used the full 86 years of yearly returns of the S&P 500 index].

Increasing to three years using a rolling-period analysis[8], the returns show less lumpiness, less variability compared to one-year returns. Randomness decreases; causality increases. In this case, the probability of losing money is 15/84 or 17.9%.

---

[8] Rolling-period analysis, based on yearly returns, is computing the CAGR (compound annualized growth rate) for three years in a row, forming all possible sequential three-year combination, like 1990, 1991, 1992 – this is one three-year combination; 1991, 1992, 1993 – another combination; etc.

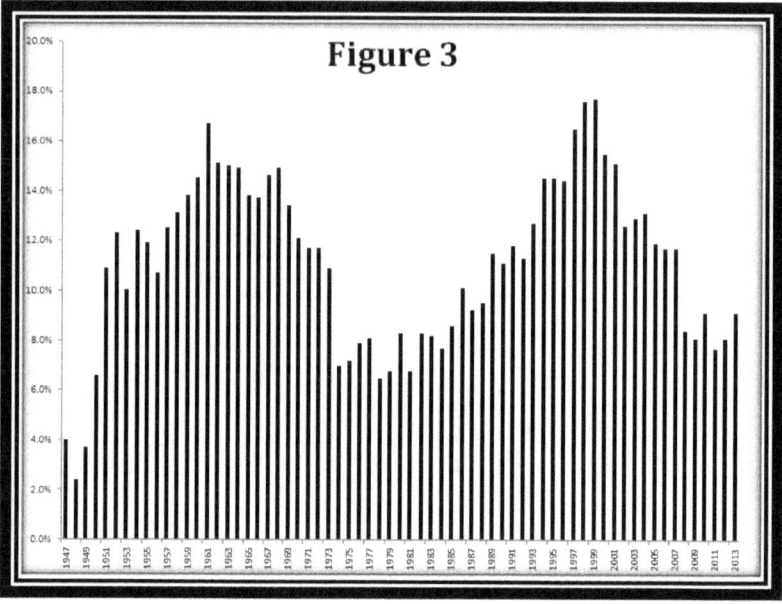

Further, increasing to five years, the returns exhibit more causality and less randomness. The probability of losing money reduces to 11/82 or 13.4%. In a 10-year holding time (see Figure 2), the probability of losing money is 5/77 or 6.49%. In a 15-year holding time, the probability of losing money is 1/72 or 1.4%. Lastly, in a 20-year holding time (see Figure 3), the probability of losing money is 0/67 or 0.0%. All 67 twenty-year rolling periods are positive.

If we continue this analysis to longer and longer times, we see a pattern emerge: as time increases, randomness decreases, while causality increases. Also, as time increases, variability decreases, as well as the probability of losing money decreases, approaching zero.

At this point, the n-year rolling period analysis yields the minimum time for holding our investment in stocks – the time when the probability of losing money is practically zero, or strictly speaking is asymptotically approaching zero. It is the time where no rolling n-year period has a negative CAGR. That time is n years. Empirically, n is about 15 years.

Existence of Portfolio Take-off

We now construct a general argument showing the waning of randomness and the waxing of causality, on their effects on stock market return. Specifically, we will show there must be a **minimum** *time* for holding our investment, in which the disruption due to randomness fades to zero effect, or a small finite value, on the cumulative return and causality rises to dominance, growing the return without limit.

Existence theorem: *there exist a minimum time in which randomness, due to cancellation in the sum of return changes, contributes zero or at most a finite value to the cumulative return; at the same time, in the absence of cancellation, causality's contribution starts to grow without limit.*

An Example of Unlimited Growth

Before we go through the argument proving the existence theorem, it is good to have an intuitive sense of the growth of return without limit. Let us examine Figure 4 and 5 together. Imagine your family held an index mutual fund that tracked the S&P 500 from 1928 to 2013. Both figures depict the cumulative return of your family portfolio. Figure 4 is a plot of the cumulative return[9] with time based on yearly returns of the S&P 500 index, from 1928 to 2013. After 86 years, the cumulative return in 2013 was so huge +255,553.3 % that the initial returns cannot show up at this scale.

---

[9] You calculate cumulative return this way: say, year 1, return is R1; year 2, return is R2; year 3, return is R3, etc. The cumulative return in year 1 is (1+R1). If you multiply the quantity with your fund, you get back your capital: your funds X 1; and the gains: your funds X R1. The cumulative return in year 3 is (1+R1)*(1+R2)*(1+R3). The same pattern holds for higher order returns.

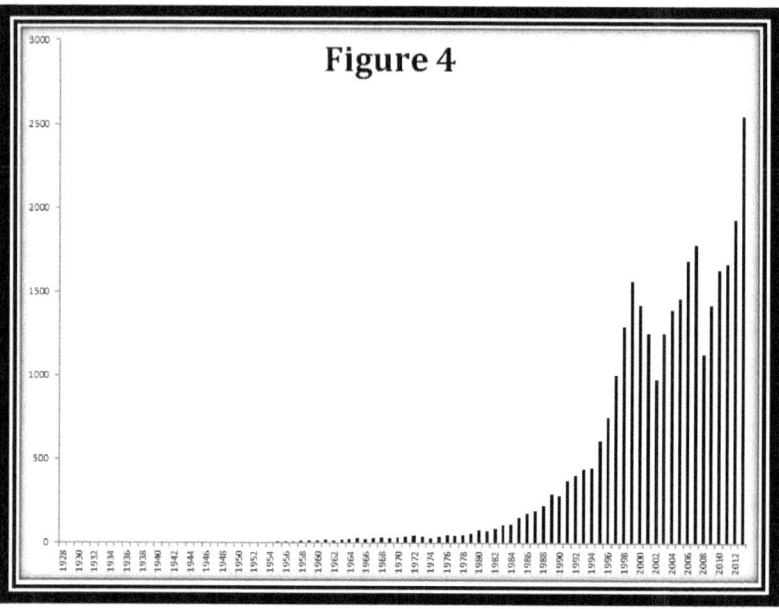

In order to see the "take-off" to growth without limits, we had to stop the graph at the 35th year, in 1962. In effect, we are zooming in on the first 35 years of the 86-year period, as shown in Figure 5. The starting year 1928 saw a stellar return of 43.8%. But, the following year witnessed the US stock market sucked into a huge black hole: four consecutive years of negative returns; four consecutive depression years: -8.3, -25.1, -43.8, and -8.6 in 1929, 1930, 1931, and 1932 respectively.

The black line in Figure 5 represented 1 or 100 %, your initial capital. Below the black line, it meant you were losing a fraction of your capital. Above the black line, it meant you were gaining capital. Notice how the US stock market struggled to raise its nose just above the water in the beginning.

For the first 15 years, from 1928 to 1942, it was bobbing above and below the surface. In the 16th year, in 1943, it started to clear the surface and never again to sink below it. In other words, the US stock market took-off in 1943; it continues to

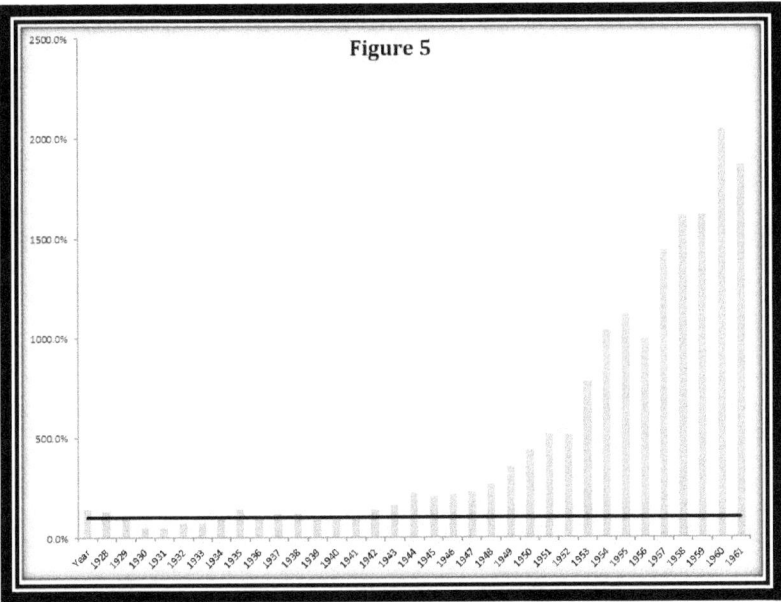

soar to the sky-is-the-limit until today and will continue in the future.

The S&P 500 index is and has been in the zone of unlimited growth. If your successive generations own a portfolio, starting in 1928, that has been tracking the S&P 500 index, then, your generational portfolio too is and has been in the zone of unlimited growth.

A portfolio in this zone continues to grow, come what may, bear markets, recession or depression. A bear market creates a dimple in the curve; but the curve goes right back up, even higher still. Look at Figure 4 again. Notice the two dimples in 2002 caused by the Dotcom bubble and in 2008 arising from the housing bubble. Note, each time the curve went right back up, even surpassing the previous peak. Once in the zone, a portfolio just rolls with the punches, so to speak, resting on the certainty as night surely follows day the stock market will recover and more.

Now that we have a specific reference for the notion of unlimited growth, we now move on to the argument proving its existence – the existence theorem.

In effect, the theory explains the upward wiggly curve of returns, like that of the S&P 500 index in Figure 4, as directly arising from the waning of randomness and the waxing of causality over time.

Proof of the Existence Theorem

We know the return changes arising from randomness can be both positive and negative. Consequently, the cumulative sum of return changes over a period, coming from randomness does not grow with time, due to the cancellation effect. At most – one way of seeing it – it is finite, bounded by, say, R – the maximum accumulated change in the return over a period, arising from randomness.

Another way of seeing it, the more practical way, is that the cumulative sum of return changes arising from randomness equals zero over the whole period in consideration. We favour this second way on the ground it is consonant with the notion of randomness. In other words, in the end, randomness effectively does not have any significant contribution to the return.

On the other hand, the return changes coming from causality can only be positive – remember, the net-buy is positive over the long term (see the previous section in this chapter, *"Definition of "net buy" over the long term"* and in chapter 1). Consequently, the cumulative sum of return changes over a period, arising from causality, because there is no cancellation, and with boost from compounding effect – grows with time without limit. Take, for example, the portfolio of Warren Buffett – it is the sky is the limit. Alternately, consider the example we discussed above: the upward rise from 1928 to 2013 of the S&P 500 index.

At this point, we see that randomness contributes zero or at most a finite amount to the return with time. On the other hand, causality's contribution grows without limit. *Therefore, we conclude there must be a length of time from the beginning, in which the portfolio starts to take-off to the sky, growing without limit.*

Two Equivalent Conditions for Take-off Time

What is this length of time from start to take-off? The following condition determines it: *when the percentage cumulative return of a portfolio is such that no negative return in future years can pull it down to a value below 100%.*

Examining the S&P 500 returns from 1928 to 2013, we find the worst patch of years is the consecutive depression years: -8.3, -25.1, -43.8, and -8.6 in 1929, 1930, 1931, and 1932 respectively. To overcome the huge downward pull of this black hole – these four consecutive negative years – our portfolio by the end of 1928 must have had a cumulative return of 183.4% just to stay outside the hole.

The black hole of 2008 was much smaller than the Depression black hole. Our portfolio only needed 57.7% to withstand the downward pull.

If history is any guide and future stock market black holes are about the magnitude of the Depression black hole, then it is safe to bet that a portfolio with a 200% cumulative return must be taking-off. In fact, it may already be cruising at a high enough altitude that no "missile" or bear market could hit it or bring it down to the ground.

Precisely because the number of consecutive negative years in the future is not known and how negative, we cannot predict the length of time until take-off from theory.

Theory can only predict the existence of portfolio take-off time, but not its specific value.

Our only recourse to get an estimate of the take-off time is to use the return data of the stock market and use the worst patch of time (to be conservative) to determine it empirically. Based on stock market data of the S&P 500 index, from 1928 to 2013, the take-off time is about 15 years. This is the **minimum** *time for holding our investment in stocks, based on the worst patch.*

The equivalent condition for the take-off time from the probability-of-losing-money view is that *the n-year rolling periods have no negative CAGR.* As we saw in the section, *Increasing Time Scales,* the minimum time for holding a portfolio is n years; where n is about 15 years.

Portfolio Take-off: Universal Property

Our analysis of the time behaviour of randomness and causality in the stock market shows the existence of a very important quantity: *portfolio take-off to unlimited growth.* It is a *universal property* of stock market returns.

We established the result above by general arguments not specific to a particular stock market. Thus, our conclusion on portfolio take-off to unlimited growth holds for all stock markets.

The basis of the last statement is the fact that the same human nature is at work in all markets, across time. The elements of the causal force – the net-buy – come from the same human nature. The net-buy springs from the same desire to provision our future by growing our money.

Portfolio take-off to unlimited growth with time is the "Holy Grail "of investing.

Who does not want their money to grow to the sky-is-the-limit?

Summary

In resume, we argued that the random part of the return does not grow with time, due to cancellation. On the other hand, we showed that the causal part of the return – in the absence of cancellation, and boosted by compounding effect – grows with time without limit.

These contrasting behaviours between randomness and causality are *universal*, in the sense they are true in all stock markets. Now, we can begin to understand why market returns always rise in a wiggly curve over the long term: *market returns always rise over the long term due to causality, with wiggles and dimples due to randomness.*

The rolling period analysis yields the minimum time for holding our stock investment. It is the time when the probability of losing money is zero or approaching zero. The S&P 500 return data yield an estimate of about 15 years.

Thus, the minimum time for holding a portfolio from the probability-of-losing-money view and the take-off time of a portfolio are the same. This means that when your odds of losing money are practically zero, your portfolio is taking-off to unlimited growth at the same time.

The following image best expresses our result: investing is like piloting a plane; portfolio takes-off after a taxi-time on the runway for about 15 years; once airborne, our portfolio ever soars to the sky-is-the-limit.

Chapter 4: Central Dogma of the Stock Market

The BIG secret is out. We solved the riddle. We unveiled the mystery. We laid bare the enigma.

A properly managed portfolio – by the very nature of the stock market, with its driving forces, randomness and causality, taking their course – at a certain point in time, will take-off to unlimited growth.

Our two-component theory of the stock market based solely on the dynamics of the forces involved confirms what the stock market is for – growing our money.

*We suggest elevating this idea – portfolio take-off to unlimited growth – to the **central dogma of the stock market**.*

Human Nature versus Nature of the Stock Market

The implication of the result above is clear: failure to attain take-off to unlimited growth falls squarely on the shoulders of the investor – on human nature, not due to ignorance of the inner workings of the stock market.

In chapter 3, we examine the nature of the forces driving the stock market. We showed take-off to unlimited growth is a natural occurrence. There are no further inner workings unknown to us, related to take-off.

Consequently, the nature of the stock market is free from blame in case of failure to attain portfolio take-off.

On the other hand, we have yet to consider human nature in view of portfolio take-off – the psychological forces driving our actions in the stock market. I lay all the faults here – the "un-naturalness" of our actions on our portfolio vis-à-vis the flow of forces driving the stock market, emanating from our primal emotions inherited from our ancestors. Our actions, prompted by randomness, delay take-off; or, may permanently "ground" our portfolio.

On the other hand, causality – the source of our return – we ignore because its effects are not visible in the short term. To do right by causality, the driving force behind our return, we should focus on the long term.

We will not discuss these issues related to human nature here any further, as we have dealt with them elsewhere: in our book, "IQ plus EQ: The Arrow and the Hoisting Crane".

Possible Psychological Impact

Here, we speculate what the psychological impact will be when people realize the "growth-without-limit" of their portfolios is a natural, as natural as growing a tree.

We suspect the psychological implication for investors is not unlike the 4-minute-mile-run impossibility barrier. Once the runner Mr Roger Bannister broke through the barrier in a sub-4-minute mile run on May 6, 1954, many others broke through the barrier as well – the psychological impossibility barrier fell off.

Similarly, the psychological impossibility barrier for many investors in achieving portfolio take-off, we predict, will also fall off, with the clear demonstration of its existence derived directly from the dynamics of the forces driving the stock market. The very nature of things dictates it, so to speak. We expect many investors will attain take-off in about 15 years from now.

Portfolio take-off is not just a Warren Buffett fluke – due to his exceptional gifts. No, portfolio take-off to unlimited growth is not a fluke. It is a natural, inevitable course if we manage our portfolio for take-off, that is, we ignore the arrow;

instead, we pay attention to the hoisting crane, as will be discussed in chapter 5.

Our analysis also shows that randomness acts like a drag on the take-off of our portfolio on the wings of causality.

Take-Off Time Depends on Actual Returns

Different portfolios will have different take-off time. The greater the CAGR of our portfolio, the sooner will our portfolio take-off to the blue yonder. Depending on the patch of time of the start and development of our portfolio, take-off time may be less than 10 years. A top performing portfolio in a patch of years very much unlike the Depression years makes it in less than 10 years.

If our portfolio underperforms the S&P 500 index, then it may take longer than 15 years to take off. However, on average, if its performance is similar to the S&P 500 index, then it takes about 15 years. Once a portfolio takes off, it will continue to grow to the sky is the limit, if properly maintained.

Many investors do not know this and miss the whole point of stock investment in the first place.

Summary

Our theory explains the universal behaviour of the stock market. The behaviour is invariant with respect to time; it is equally invariant with respect to location. The imprint of invariance traces from the fact that *Homo sapiens* remains the same throughout the ages and across geographies. As we will see in the Appendix, in the final analysis, intentionality is the causality driving the stock market, while the un-coordinated execution of that intentionality is the randomness driving the stock market at the same time.

Universality or invariance, the nature of *Homo sapiens,* and intentionality are the ultimate notions on which our understanding of the behaviour of the stock market rests.

It is appropriate to elevate portfolio take-off to unlimited growth as the *Central Dogma of the Stock Market.*

Chapter 5: The Arrow and the Hoisting Crane

"Metaphors have a way of holding the most truth in the least space."
Orson Scott Card

"Metaphors are much more tenacious than facts."
Paul de Man

We now bring all the elements of our theory and their ramifications into focus with this image: **the arrow and the hoisting crane.**

The image is an intuitive picture of the whole theory. The small arrow represents tiny effects – the effects of randomness on returns. The elevated hoisting crane represents tall structures – the ever-rising curve of returns coming from causality. It is easy to carry with us. It is ever ready to use anytime.

A Sentiment Device

Imagine a small arrow with its pivot attached to a rope hung from a tall hoisting crane. The arrow rotates about its pivot. The hoisting crane slowly lifts or lowers the pivot, by winding or unwinding the rope in slow motion, as the whole device moves to the right with time.

This device mirrors the short-term and the long-term sentiments of investors.

Randomness is the arrow. The arrow rotates to point up or down at every buy or sell. It rotates like crazy—as many millions of times as the number of buys or sells daily. The arrow has a built-in intelligence that computes the daily return.

It passes the daily return to the hoisting crane. Note the return computed takes into account the compounding growth effect. Essentially, compounding comes from the fact that we roll forward the total amount—the original + the gains. We buy shares using the total amount. Therefore, when the arrow computes the daily return, it takes account of all shares bought by the initial amount plus all the gains at a point in time. At the end of a trading day, the arrow points either up or down, with length proportional to the return.

What is the role of the hoisting crane? We will view the hoisting crane in two ways: the "integral" view or the bird's eye view – like the optimal path between two points; and the "differential" view or the detailed view – like the point-by-point changes in a curve.

The "Integral" View of the Hoisting Crane

Causality is the hoisting crane in the "integral" view. Remember the element of the causal force is the net-buy over the long term. Remember, too, the cumulative sum of the changes in return arising from randomness does not grow with time; they add up to zero, or at most to a small finite value. Furthermore, beyond the take-off point, the return is virtually from causality. The upshot of all this is that we can ignore the effect of randomness on the motion of the hoisting crane or the return, over a long period.

To drive home the point, we can calibrate the motion of the hoisting crane in accord with the CAGR for the whole period. By so doing, we are tracing the effective curve determined by the average growth rate for the period. For the sake of argument, grant special powers to the computing unit in the hoisting crane to "smell" from the initial path the total path for the whole period. Then, the computing unit knows the initial and the final value of the portfolio, calculates the CAGR, and moves the pivot accordingly.

Thus, the curve traced in the return-time space is a smooth curve – the effects of randomness drop out in the integral view– arching upwards along the return axis. This is what we mean when we say that causality is the hoisting crane.

It is not outlandish to suppose the "integral" view of the optimal path natural processes take. Nature seems to like it. Light, for example, seems to know (to "smell") the path that takes the optimal time. We know that light naturally follows the path of least time.

Similarly, we grant the hoisting crane knows the effective CAGR right at the beginning, and calibrate its motion accordingly.

The View Through the CAGR-lens

Another name for the integral view is the CAGR-lens. When we think of our returns, we should think through the lens of CAGR. Then, we see clearly what is happening or what will or should happen. The practice of choosing a benchmark for comparison with your portfolio performance shows the importance of the CAGR view.

The name of the game is to beat the market, or the benchmark representing the market. If we choose the S&P 500 index as our benchmark, then the game is to beat the 9.6% compound annualized growth rate it registered from 1928 to 2013.

To beat the 9.6% CAGR of the S&P 500 index, we have to populate our portfolio with stocks whose shares other investors will buy more. We have to think how to increase the net-buy of stocks in our portfolio to increase our return.

In the integral or the CAGR view, we forget about the arrow, the random force – it does not figure at all in this view. The CAGR view promotes the correct management of our portfolio, by ignoring the arrow and focusing on the hoisting crane. Our concern is how we can increase the speed of the hoisting crane (to raise the CAGR), thereby raising the pivot up the most.

The "Differential" View of the Hoisting Crane

The "differential" view takes account of what happens at each point in time. The hoisting crane has a built-in intelligence that computes the running cumulative return based on information passed on by the arrow. It hoists the pivot up or lowers it down according to the running cumulative return at the set time scale. The crane moves the pivot to the right with time.

We set the parts of our device according to their natural time scale: the arrow we set in seconds, the hoisting crane in decades.

A typical scene is the following. On any trading day, we witness the arrow furiously rotating—to point up, or, to point down. However, the pivot hardly moves at all. The hoisting motion of the crane moves extremely slowly with its time scale set in decades. The slow, if majestic motion of the hoisting crane, tells us it is foolish to act on the time scale of the arrow.

We should realize the stark contrast of the realities depicted by each component of our sentiment device. The snail-paced motion of the hoisting crane represents the cumulative return. The squirrel-hurry rotation of the arrow corresponds to the random motion of the return.

To the detriment of our portfolio, the arrow hijacks our attention. First, the time scale of the arrow is commensurate with our own time scale, ranging from a second to a day. Second, what the arrow reveals in the short-term fluctuation is emotionally disturbing to us.

Unfortunately, for the reasons cited above, the arrow is the center of our emotional concern and response.

On the other hand, due to its slow motion or its long time scale, many investors do not pay attention to the hoisting crane. Our time horizon is so short we find difficulty in taking a long-term view.

Sentiments, Boom and Bust

The long-term sentiment is present; it is most of the time positive. However, more or less at regular intervals, the positive sentiment builds up over a long time to a peak. Then, for some reason, triggered by fear, the positive sentiment turns negative in a relatively short time, except for a few rich, who are very positive and bullish, buying the whole stock market on sale.

Our hoisting crane unwinds the tether furiously, sending the pivot in a free fall. Upon reaching its lowest point, the crane usually jerks the pivot up by a quick winding of the rope. So goes the story of the stock market boom and bust.

Transfers of wealth from the poor to the rich

What do all these mean in terms of people, in terms of you or us? What we have just described are the **great transfers of wealth in bear markets,** from those who do not have much to those who already have so much! Remember, for every seller, there is a buyer.

In a massive sell-off, an ordinary investor – who does not know much about the nature of the stock market and therefore vulnerable to fear and greed, envy and herd mentality—sells his shares at great discount of his purchase price. He is selling to someone on the other side of the transaction who knows much about the stock market and who has tons and tons of money just waiting for such an opportunity.

To put it crudely, but rather accurately—a bear market is a massive transfer of wealth from the poor to the rich! The recent example was the 2007-2009 bear market!

They say great wealth changes hands in a bear market. However, whose hands—from whose hand to whose hand?

Just a thought: if everybody holds on to his/her stocks, there will be no massive sell-off and thus no massive transfer of wealth!

This is the pipe dream of this book!

Summary

In resume the image of the small arrow and the tall hoisting crane is packed full of ideas of our theory of the stock market. The arrow stands for randomness; its smallness, the small effect of randomness on returns. The hoisting crane stands for causality; its tallness, the ever-rising curve of returns with time.

The image is also a "summary" guide to managing our portfolio – ignore the arrow; focus attention on the hoisting crane.

In effect, we have separated the random, the arrow, from the causal, the hoisting crane – in accord with our two-component theory of stock market return.

Chapter 6: Consequences of the Theory

This chapter presents the important consequences flowing from the theory. First is its implication on our psychology – our attitude toward the stock market. Second is its implication on our investing approach. Third is the implication of the theory on portfolio management.

We close the chapter with some parting thoughts.

Attitude toward the Stock Market

"Let things flow naturally forward in whatever way they like".
Lao Tzu

A key consequence of our theory is the overall attitude we should have toward the stock market – encapsulated by the quote from the Chinese philosopher Lao Tzu.

"Let things flow naturally forward in whatever way they like" is to go with the flow of the forces driving the stock market. In other words, we sidestep the negative force of randomness and ride on the positive force of causality.

As we said in the Introduction, growing our money in the stock market is no different from growing a tree in our garden. We grow a tree not in disregard of, but in conformity with its nature. We grow our money in the stock market, not by opposing, but by going with the flow dynamics of the forces.

Long-time Nature of Investing

The first thing a beginning investor must realize is the long-time nature of investing in the stock market. Investing in stocks is not a quick fix; neither is it a hit-and-run affair. Fifteen years is a very long time, indeed! The sooner we free ourselves from the get-rich-quick myths surrounding investing, the better it will be for us.

The natural flow of the forces driving the stock market sets the pace of investing. Do not meet force with force, but deflect it to throw your foe off-balance, so goes a practice from the martial arts. That is exactly what we have to do in the stock market.

Letting the Causal Force Take our Money

We invest to grow our money. From our theory, two forces influence that growth: the random force and the causal force. The random force impedes the growth, while the causal force grows our money.

We cannot avoid the random force. We may directly confront it to our detriment, as countless investors find their portfolios underperforming the benchmark – without their understanding why. However, Kung Fu-like, we can weave our steps around it, while time renders it powerless. This means we have to wait for about 15 years, when time finally subdues it to insignificance, while allowing the causal force to rise in dominance.

If we are able to hold our portfolio and ourselves until randomness becomes "forceless", then we can hand our money to the causal force to grow it and never again worry about the random force.

Many of us, instead of getting past the random force to hand our money to the causal force to grow it, are stuck fighting the random force. Nobody can beat the random force. Leave the random force alone. Do not respond to "correct" its fluctuations.

The Whole Point of Investing

With a clear picture of the forces at work, we realize the stock market is not what it seems. We may describe it at two levels: the surface phenomena and below-the-surface reality. The frenetic up-down rotation of the arrow – the daily alternation of "red" and "green" numbers in our portfolio – is a "mask" covering our return. We readily see the surface optics without thinking. Unfortunately, many of us have only a vague idea beyond the distorted optics.

On the other hand, the "Holy Grail" of investing can only be "seen" by thinking, rather than by physical sight: **portfolio take-off** *to unlimited growth.* The time scale difference between a second and a decade tells us, how far removed the "thing", we are really after, from the thing screaming for our attention.

The slow, if majestic almost imperceptible motion of the hoisting crane is indicative of the remoteness of our goal – many steps removed from the daily emotions stirred by our portfolio, from the daily frenetic stirrings of the arrow.

Patience is the virtue most necessary for investors. Investing is like piloting a plane that taxis on the runway for about 15 years and then takes-off to unlimited growth. In the context of our short time horizon, a wait of 15 years is a very long time, indeed. Nevertheless, portfolio take-off to unlimited growth is the whole point of investing in the stock market in the first place.

Psychologically, who among us can wait for 15 years for an alleged take-off of our portfolio? We hope our proof will help investors stay the course, a rather long one, unfortunately. We proved that (1) it exists, as we demonstrated with the S&P 500 index from 1928 to 2013; corroborated by successful investors like Warren Buffett; and (2) if we do not stand in the way, it is a natural outcome of the forces driving the stock market.

There is simply no royal road to riches!

Portfolio take-off should be the topic of conversation of investors. Portfolio take-off should be the goal of every investor. Portfolio take-off should be the reason why anyone invests in the stock market at all.

Investing Approach

We move on to examine the impact of the theory on our investing approach.

Our returns depend on the choice of stocks we populate our portfolio. Our choice, in turn, depends on our investing approach. Many viable investing approaches are in use. The most famous approach is the buy-and-hold, pioneered by Phillip Fisher and made visible to the public at large by Warren Buffett. This approach requires the ability to make sound valuations of businesses.

A similar buy-and-hold approach with a difference in the specific method in evaluating stocks for inclusion (not the standard valuation of discounted streams of earnings in the lifetime of the company) has recently received attention through two books, lectures and seminars by Phil Town.

Another approach is Greenblatt's magic formula investing approach. This approach we described in some detail in our book:" IQ plus EQ: The Arrow and the Hoisting Crane."

Many more investing approaches are viable. What we are interested in demonstrating in this section, are the general arguments in choosing an investing approach, based on our theory.

Our theory says the only way to increase the motion of the hoisting crane, thereby increasing our return, is to increase the net-buy over the long term. This means that other investors will buy more shares of the stocks populating our portfolio.

To repeat, the stocks we populate our portfolio are crucial to attaining take-off. The net-buy by other investors of shares of stocks in our portfolio is what drives the hoisting crane, i.e. our return.

How does that happen? The hoisting crane metaphor provides the framework for the answer. Increasing our return implies increasing the speed of the hoisting crane. In turn, this means increasing the net-buy of shares of stocks in our portfolio. In turn, this means other investors see our portfolio as full of bargain stocks. In turn, this means we bought our stocks with a margin of safety or paid a lot less; and instead of buying ordinary companies, we bought above average companies at below average prices.

Our theory provides a natural entry for the two perennial principles of sound investing to the question of how best to ride the causal force driving the hoisting crane. The principles are Benjamin Graham's principle of margin of safety; and Warren Buffett's principle of buying companies at below average prices is good, but buying good companies at below average prices is even better.

If we buy companies with a margin of safety, i.e. at a price lower than their fair value—paying a lot less—on average, statistically speaking, the number of net buys, and the amount of each net-buy of stocks in our portfolio by other investors are greater than when we buy shares at or above their fair or intrinsic value.

Remember the net-buy over the long term is what sets the motion of the hoisting crane.

There is greater demand on stocks perceived as priced below their fair value. The prices of said stocks rise by this mechanism. It may take time for other investors to see the situation as a bargain.

We assume that eventually investors will agree the stocks we pick populating our portfolio are below their fair value, irrespective of whether they represent ordinary or good companies. On average, many are likely to buy and in greater number of shares. How long shall we wait for other investors to agree with us?

The last question brings us to a decision crossing, which will be different for different investing approaches. The buy-and-hold approach, for example, will hold stocks for a very long time.

In the Greenblatt approach, which we use, we take a statistical compromise—we hold our stocks for one year.

Stocks are like fruits; they ripen at different times. In a portfolio of 20 to 30 stocks, we expect a distribution of "ripening" or of rising to fair value over a time. Some reach their fair value less than a year, some others, more than a year. To eliminate the emotion in the process of determining which stocks reach what fair value, one may adopt a compromise: a cut through with a statistical knife, setting the time of harvest to one year.

Furthermore, if we buy good companies at below average prices, then, on average, the same result above is statistically expected: the number of net-buys and the amount of each net-buy are greater compared to the case of buying at or above their intrinsic or fair value—even more so, compared with the previous case. Now, we have good companies, instead of just ordinary companies, at prices below their fair value.

The demand for stocks is even greater for the case of good companies than the case of ordinary companies.

Mr. Market supplies unduly bid-down stocks

How do opportunities like those above arise? Why do prices of companies go down below their fair value, thereby enabling us to apply the *first principle* of sound investing: the *"margin of safety"* principle? There are always stocks with prices that are unduly high, as well as unduly low, as Graham used to point out using Mr. Market as a metaphor for the psychology of investors.

How is it so? When a company misses analysts' earnings estimate, which to begin with is at best questionable, investors tend to overreact. With our bias to loss aversion, as well as to fear, we tend to overreact to bad news. Investors who hold shares of the said company may dump their shares sending the price unduly down, much worse than what the fundamentals of the company underlying the stock truly reflect.

On the other hand, when a company for some reason receives much favorable attention from the press, and/or hyped reports, such as Microsoft in the making, or the next Apple; or the management runs the company extremely well, etc.—with our bias to believe and to greed, many of us form an exaggerated regard for the said company. We look at the company in much better light than what its fundamentals are saying. In our list of choices, we find ourselves ranking the said company as our first pick. Many of us will buy shares of the said company bidding the price unduly up.

Where does this lead us? To the conclusion, at any time: (1) there are unduly bid-down stocks, arising from our biases of fear and aversion to loss; (2) there are unduly bid-up stocks, due to our biases to believe exaggerated reports and to greed; and (3) we have to develop a method of finding out especially the unduly bid down stocks.

If we can find a systematic way of discovering the unduly bid-down stocks, then we can comply with the first principle—the margin of safety, or, paying a lot less. This means we will only have in our portfolio unduly bid-down stocks. We are paying for them a lot less. We have a margin of safety.

However, wait. Is an unduly bid-down stock or a cheap stock always undeserving of its low price? Do many unduly bid-down stocks not deserve the sentiment with which investors regard them?

Principle: buying good companies at below average prices

Beware buyer! Many cheap stocks are cheap because they deserve it. This brings us to the **second principle** of sound investing from Warren Buffett. He remarked buying companies at below average prices is good; but *buying good companies at below average prices is even better.*

The algorithm for our search is to look for unduly bid down stocks and choose the good companies among them; or, equally, look for good companies and choose only the unduly bid-down stocks among them. We will populate our portfolio, using this search formula.

At this point, we agree on the conceptual criteria for our choice of stocks/companies—cheap and good. We believe our criteria of cheap and good, i.e. good companies bought below fair value, enable us to ride the causal or drift force optimally, thereby optimizing our returns—sending the hoisting motion of the crane up the most.

We now have to translate the concept of "cheap" and the concept of "good" into quantitative properties for convenient comparison to facilitate our search.

The specific translations of what is "cheap" and what is "good" spell out the different investing approaches. [For more details on the Greenblatt approach, see our book, "IQ plus EQ: The Arrow and the Hoisting Crane"].

Investing in index funds

For those of us who are not comfortable picking stocks or managing a portfolio, investing in an index fund is the way to go. However, be aware mutual funds do not perform equally. Among index or passive mutual funds, we have four categories: market-capitalization weighted, equally weighted, fundamentally weighted, and value weighted funds. The majority of funds are market-cap weighted. An example of a market-cap weighted index is the S&P 500. Market-cap weighted funds yield the lowest performance among the four categories. The top performer is the value weighted index funds.

The reason for the lower performance of the market-cap weighted index is that it doubles down on the market distortions arising from fear and greed. It owns more of the unduly bid-up stocks arising from greed; at the same time, it owns less of the unduly bid-down stocks arising from fear – because of its very structure.

The desirable composition of a fund should be just the opposite: own less of the unduly bid-up stocks and more of the unduly bid-down stocks. The value-weighted fund is one-step better – it owns only unduly bid-down stocks. This is the reason for its higher returns.

Managing a Portfolio for Take-off

"For investors as a whole, returns decrease as motion increases."
Warren Buffett

In the quote above, Warren Buffett alludes to the "hyper-activity" of investors in the management of their portfolios. Motion increases as we respond to the promptings of the arrow. For as long as we ignore the hoisting crane, but, instead, yield to the temptations coming from the arrow – such as change from one mutual fund to another, or go in and out of stocks to time the market – our portfolios will not take-off.

Ignore the Arrow; Focus on the Hoisting Crane

The arrow and the hoisting crane is a convenient "summary" guide in managing our portfolio: ignore the arrow; focus on the hoisting crane. It cannot be simpler than that.

This is a key consequence of the theory.

To act on the promptings of the arrow, say replacing some offending stocks, to have higher return (equivalent to changing the motion of the hoisting crane), is to act on the wrong driving force. The actions of the arrow are essentially independent from those of the hoisting crane. To influence the hoisting crane, we must act directly on it.

What aspect of the hoisting crane should we focus on? The speed of the hoisting crane should be our concern: is the speed optimal? We know the net-buy over the long term is the causal force driving the motion of the hoisting crane. Thus, from our theory, the only avenue of optimizing the speed of the hoisting crane is to optimize the net-buy over the long term.

How do we do that? The answer brings us to the next section.

Aim to Take-off

As posed in the last section, what is the point of investing in stocks if we do not aim for take-off? All our actions should have one goal: to achieve portfolio take-off. That is the real pay-off from investing in stocks.

Managing a portfolio, then, is like piloting a plane and we are the pilot. We know the taxi time on the runway is about 15 years. We intend to climb to the sky in a shorter time. Since we are the pilot, we must attend to the factors critical to be airborne sooner:

1. The design of the plane is crucial.

2. The correct operation of the controls of the plane is indispensable.

In terms of investing, the first factor refers to the choice of stocks populating our portfolio. We make sure our choice of stocks populating our portfolio is in accord with the two perennial principles of sound investing. By so doing, we optimize the net-buy over the long term. See section on *Investing Approach* above.

The second factor refers to the correct management of our portfolio, i.e. ignore the arrow and focus on the hoisting crane. We will not discuss portfolio management here as we have covered it elsewhere in our book, "IQ plus EQ: The Arrow and the Hoisting Crane", including an exposition on the main obstacle standing in the way to success in the stock market – human nature.

Thinking we are the pilot of our portfolio, doing everything, we can to get airborne in the shortest possible time makes investing an exciting activity, as well as focuses the mind on what really matters.

Why Buffett Succeeds, while Others Fail?

"Only buy something that you'd be perfectly happy to hold if the market shut down for 10 years."
Warren Buffett

Why do not all portfolios attain take-off? Why do some attain it? Why do others fail?

In the framework of our theory, most investors focus their attention on the arrow, and not on the hoisting crane. That in so many words is the answer to why Buffett succeeds, while others fail.

Note the implications of the Buffett quote above. First, in accord with the theory, Buffett has not paid any attention to the arrow, or to short-term events. Second, he focuses on the natural time scale of the hoisting crane, which is reflective of the time scale of portfolio returns – in decades.

In contrast to what Warren Buffett does, many of us ignore the hoisting crane; instead, we pay attention to the random, short-term events of our portfolio. We do something, anything – resulting in excessive buys and sells – actions that do not contribute to the cause of achieving portfolio take-off.

These actions, instead, are equivalent to drilling holes in the wings of our portfolio disabling its take-off.

Success has a simple formula. Populate our portfolio with stocks according to our chosen investing approach. Manage our portfolio by ignoring the arrow and paying attention to the hoisting crane. Repeat until take-off.

Parting Thoughts

We tend to compartmentalize our experiences. That group of reality is the "financial markets", wholly different from this group of reality we call "living organisms", etc. Seeing differences in things similar and similarities in things different are two modes of thinking.

In our parting thoughts, we show the similarity between the "push to grow" in the stock market and the "push to grow" in a shoot.

The image of a shoot naturally pushing to grow is a good reminder of what our attitude should be toward investing. Surrounding the shoot are the forces of entropy or disorder. Nevertheless, it may successfully negotiate crossing the threshold to viability and onward to full maturity. Many others do not meet the same success.

The shoot illustrates the natural flow of the forces driving plant growth, and other processes in Nature. On one side, we have what Bergson called the *Élan vital* or in modern biology, we call the DNA – pushing the shoot to grow. On the other side, we have the entropic forces tending to disrupt the growing-up process.

We happen to view the stock market, as having the same type of forces, as well as the same type of dynamics overall, as a shoot has. On one hand, we have "the push to grow" our money coming from the desire to provision our future, making the net-buy greater in magnitude than the net-sell over time. On the other hand, retarding "the push to grow" are the entropic or random forces pulling in the opposite direction.

A plant sidesteps the requirement of the second law of thermodynamics by releasing disorder to its surroundings greater than the decrease in disorder the plant internally uses to go on living – thereby satisfying the requirement of the second law of entropy or disorder increase.

Similarly, to cross the threshold to unlimited growth, we have to sidestep the effect of randomness on our return by simply doing nothing to "correct" it – which is extremely difficult for the offspring of dwellers in the savannahs in Africa – letting time do the subduing of randomness for us.

Yes, it takes time. Fifteen years or so, indeed, is a long time. However, we cannot command the forces to flow differently. The force flows have their natural time scales. Our investing approach, as well as the managing of our portfolio, has to conform to the natural flows of the forces driving the stock market.

Due to our weakness in statistical reasoning – we are poor intuitive statistician – the pre-take-off stage is fraught with difficulties for investors, the first 15 years or so. Lacking an intuitive understanding of random events, we fail to see the fluctuations in our return for what they are – random, thereby requiring no action. However, we feel compelled to act, to do something, anything in response to the randomly rotating arrow, up or down resulting in the "green" or "red" numbers in our portfolio.

The words of Warren Buffett express precisely the reason why investors have low returns and thus fail to attain take-off. *"For investors as a whole, returns decrease as motion increases"*.

Post take-off, causality dominates and randomness fades into the background. We are now solely dealing with a positive force. It is a lot easier on our emotions. We deserve a celebration on reaching this stage – the zone of unlimited growth.

As a last thought, we ask what the ideal time horizon is for investing. The logic of the theory points to the answer: *forever*. To repeat, the time horizon ideal for investing in stocks is forever. This entails that portfolio stewardship pass from one generation to the next. We should all aim for this ideal.

Conclusion: What it means to Investors

The achievement of Warren Buffett without any doubt is extraordinary. Our theory does not take any lustre away from the spectacular way he achieved it. Buffett had no negative years, from 1965 to 1997. His portfolio literally took-off right from the start.

What our theory asserts is that the attainment of portfolio take-off to unlimited growth is a natural, as natural as growing a tree in our garden. Anyone with an average IQ and above average EQ (emotional intelligence) can attain it. Unlike Buffett, we may stumble along the way. The time to attain it may be longer. Nevertheless, attainment it is just the same – if we pass the take-off point.

To those of us who are not comfortable picking stocks or managing a portfolio, investing in index fund is the way to go. The example we used in the book is the S&P 500 index. It attained take-off after 15 years, starting in 1928, around the Great Depression. We will do much better than the S&P 500 index by choosing a value-weighted index fund. Greenblatt has shown value-weighted funds perform yearly 5% above the performance of market-capitalization weighted index funds.

If we stay invested in a value-weighted index fund, we will likely attain take-off earlier than 15 years.

To those of us who are comfortable picking stocks or managing a portfolio, there are many paths to attain portfolio take-off. The multiplicity of paths can be a source of doubt as to the best or the shortest. Each of us has to resolve this issue.

We leave you with this image. Investing is like piloting a plane. Our portfolio takes-off after a taxi time of about 15 years. Once airborne, it will continue to climb to the sky-is-the-limit.

Epilogue: Human Understanding

Mathematics or the quantitative approach came later in human evolution. Qualitative thinking, on the other hand, long pre-dated it. To our mind, this possibly may indicate our greater capacity in qualitative thinking compared to a quantitative one.

We hope this book will serve as an example to inspire others who have a poetic bent of mind to pursue qualitative explanations of the still many unsolved questions. Equally, we hope the book will instil courage among those who think qualitatively, to stand up and feel equal to and no intimidation from quantitative thinkers.

This is not to denigrate the importance of quantitative thinking. Just think of the invention of the Calculus. The point we want to stress is that humans should use all the arsenals at their disposal. We should cultivate a non-prejudicial attitude. Prejudice is a disadvantage: it closes possibilities.

We suspect that prejudice for a mathematical approach to "solving" the problem of explaining the stock market derailed attempts at solutions. We pursued the idea of explaining the stock market, without prejudice to any approach.

As in many other aspects in life, to be open is to be a step toward a solution.

Let us all use both qualitative and quantitative thinking in confronting the remaining unsolved mysteries.

Appendix

Axiomatic Presentation of the Theory

To see clearly the whole, as it were, in one glance, we give below an axiomatic presentation of the theory, in terms of postulates and their consequences.

Postulates:

1. Return is a composite: a random and a causal part.

2. The random part arises from the un-coordinated executions of buy and sell, by tens of millions of investors.

3. The causal part comes from the net-buy over the long term, by investors anticipating share-price appreciation, based on the expected continuing economic growth worldwide.

4. The change in return coming from the random part can be positive or negative; consequently, its cumulative sum does not grow with time because of cancellation: it is zero or at most a small finite value.

5. The change in return arising from the causal part is positive; consequently, in the absence of cancellation, its cumulative sum, boosted by compound growth effect, grows with time without limit.

Consequences:

1. Directly, from postulate four and five, there must be a time when causality's contribution to return starts to pull away from that of randomness, growing the return with time without limit. We call this time the portfolio take-off time to unlimited growth.

2. The whole point of investing in stocks is to achieve take-off.

3. The length of the take-off time is beyond deduction from the postulates. Stock market return data can give an estimate: it is about 15 years.

4. Our theory through postulate 3, gives a framework for choosing the investing approach, among the many viable approaches. There is only one criterion for the candidate approach to meet: which of the viable approaches best rides the causal force?

5. Consequence 3 shows the long-time nature of investment in the stock market. Investors should disabuse their minds of the quick-rich myths surrounding stock investing: the sooner, the better for their portfolio.

Compound Growth

Nature exhibits compound growth in the population of organisms, a process that is usually benign, sometimes troublesome. A dangerous kind, which to this day poses a threat to a possible annihilation of humankind, is the population growth of nuclei undergoing fission in a chain reaction.

In this section, we present intuitive arguments to explain compound growth.

Compound Growth: from cell to full-grown you

The best way to think about compound growth is your self-growth. A full grown you has about 37.2 trillion cells. Simplifying the complex situation, by simply asking approximately how many cell divisions you underwent to make you. Doing the calculation, we get about 45 cell divisions. From a microscopic fertilized egg, it took the egg just 45 cell divisions to make you.

In the same way, a small amount of money in 40-45 years of compound growth will balloon to a huge amount, like you from a microscopic size ballooning to an adult human in merely 45 cell divisions.

At compound annual growth rate of 12%, (the average return of the S&P 500 index is about 12%), an investment of $5,000 at this rate will become $465,255 in 40 years. At the compound rate of 17%, $5,000 will become $2,669,344 in 40 years. That is a lot of growth of your money!

There is a point in time when the annual incremental growth of your portfolio is bigger than your annual expenditure. At this point, you can start to withdraw a set amount, say your quarterly expenditure, leaving a core amount that continues to grow for a long time.

Compound Growth: rabbit population explosion

You may ask how the "drift" component of returns grows at a compound rate. That is an excellent question. A way to understand a compound rate of growth of your return is to see the growth of a rabbit population starting from a rabbit pair.

We simplify the process of rabbit breeding for the purpose of this comparison. The original pair gives birth to first generation baby rabbits. Then, the original pair and the first generation give birth to next generation and so on. After a finite number of cycles, we have a population of rabbits exploding in number.

When we have a quantity that grows in proportion to itself and itself consists of the original self + growth—then what we have is an *explosive* growth. In Finance, we call it- compounded growth. To sound mathematical, we call it *exponential* growth.

Understanding compound growth may help allay some of our concerns. As we noted above, more investors are positive about the future of the world Economy. They see the future demand for goods and services worldwide will continue to grow, due to the continued growth of the world population. This implies the net-buy is greater in magnitude than the net-sell over a period. The net increment in a year, say, is positive.

In rabbit language, our original investment gives "birth" to some gains.

This net positive increment plus the original amount we roll over to the next year. In rabbit language, this is like the original pair plus the first born-litter going for the next breeding cycle. One of two things will happen—the rolled amount gains either a net positive increment, or a negative increment.

In rabbit language, we continue to invest the original amount + gain in the second year—either giving "birth" to new gains; or no gains at all, in fact losing some of the rolled amount.

Let us take the positive case first. The total amount of the first year (the initial capital plus the positive increment) produces a positive increment in the second year. This process repeats as long as we hold our portfolio.

Our investment money grows exactly as our simplified rabbits grow—an EXPLOSIVE growth—over time!

We now take the second case: the increment in the second year is negative. The total amount of the first year plus the negative increment in the second year is an amount lower than the total amount at the end of the first year. We roll the smaller amount in the third year and so on.

In rabbit language, the effect of a negative return is to reduce the number of breeding rabbits, thereby reducing the cumulative total from which to continue the next cycle.

The effect of positive and negative increments—remember in the long run, the net sum is positive—what we see as we follow the return annually is a quantity that meanders up and down the return landscape. However, eventually, over the long term, say 20 years or more, the overall net effect is a bigger quantity compared to the initial amount. We can characterize the overall growth of our money, from the initial to the final, by a constant average growth rate over the total holding period—the CAGR: compound annualized growth rate of, say, 15%.

As long as more investors are optimistic about the future than pessimistic, the net-buy is greater in magnitude than the net-sell. As long as humanity is around—then whatever may come, economic boom or bust, recession or depression, the stock market, a leading indicator of the Economy, like Phoenix, will rise from the ashes and ever grows as rabbits grow.

In summary, stock market returns have two components—a random and a causal or "drift" upward component. The random buy and sell generate the lumpy returns. We directly see and feel this lumpiness—this is what we see and feel daily in our portfolio. It is the source of grief and mistakes to many of us.

On the other hand, the net-buy and the compound growth of the corresponding net amount over the long-term causes the upward "drift" component. We do not see, nor feel this upward drift. The drift upward is hard to see in the short term; but could be surprisingly HUGE over a long enough time.

Intentionality Lights up the Stock Market

Randomness versus Causality is a daily drama we play in the stock market. The majority of investors, however, are unaware they are the Randomness, as well as the Causality.

Let me explain.

We have seen in the previous chapters that the return of the stock market is the result of the interplay between two protagonists – causality and randomness. The source of randomness in the stock market is easy to visualize. The uncoordinated buying and selling of shares of stocks by tens of millions of investors worldwide in time and amounts – we easily see as random.

However, the net-buy over the long term is harder to visualize. For, in fact, ultimately, the causal force powering the stock market is *intentionality.*

The "net-buy over the long term" is one to three steps removed from what we directly sense. The thought of buying shares of stocks based on our perception of the Economy – is a step removed from our senses.

The thought of buying shares of stocks based on our perception that other investors will buy shares on the continued growth of the Economy – is two steps removed from what we feel with our senses.

The thought of buying shares based on our perception that other investors' anticipation of share-price rise due to the buying of shares by other investors seeing the economic trend of growth in the future – is three steps removed from our sense data.

The anticipation of share-price rise in the future by investors at different levels of intentionality is the reason for stock market return.

Intentionality, at least at three levels, drives the return of the stock market.

The execution, however, of investors' intentionality is uncoordinated. Both the time of execution and the amount of shares purchased or sold have a random distribution.

Thus, we can look at the random part of stock market return, as well, in a new light. The uncoordinated execution of investors' intentionality results in the randomness of returns.

The causal force is *intentionality;* the random force is *the uncoordinated execution* of that intentionality. That is the stuff of the stock market.

Thus, we are the Causality, as well as the Randomness, both powering the stock market.

It is no wonder why psychology plays an important role in the stock market. Intentionality makes the stock market. Intentionality is the stuff we have to deal with, the stuff within us – our own psychology that determines our behaviour in the stock market, the stuff within others – their psychology that determines their behaviour in the stock market.

Throughout the book, we explored the forces driving the stock market, chasing their dynamic behaviour in the space of return and time – only to end up where we started – us.

We have come full circle. The famous words of the poet T. S. Eliot aptly describe our situation, and we quote:

"We shall not cease from exploration, and the end of our exploring will be to arrive where we started and know the place for the first time".

About the Author

Feliciano Bantilan earned his AB Philosophy from St Francis Xavier Major Seminary, Davao City, Philippines. After his MS Physics from University of the Philippines at Diliman, Quezon City, he went to the USA on fellowship to pursue a PhD in Physics. He obtained his PhD in Physics from Duke University in 1983. He returned to his country and taught Physics at the University of the Philippines at Los Banos.

Then, a bombshell dropped on his life: Parkinson's disease in 2002. The lowest point in his struggle with Parkinson's occurred in 2006, when his mobility was so impaired, he no longer could raise himself up on bed to sleep. He slept on a mattress spread on the floor. He would have episodes of near panic, due to difficulty breathing. Then, by a stroke of luck, still with severe movement difficulty--only a finger in his left hand could press keys of his laptop--he chanced upon the website of Dr Amy Yasko.

A year and three months into her protocol, he began to get back some of his mobility, as well as some of his "brain". In addition, something more: all of a sudden, he began to think in verse. He enjoyed reading and reciting poetry since he was young. However, he never composed a poem in his life, until his partial recovery. At age sixty-five, he began writing poetry. The first two poems he composed made up his first book published in 2013, *Einstein in Verse: Introduction to Special and General Relativity*. The rest formed the content of his second book published in 2014, *Life in Poetry: The Evolutionary 'Garden of Eden'*. He published his third book written this time in prose, *IQ plus EQ: The Arrow and the Hoisting Crane,* on June 10, 2014. This is his fourth book, *Portfolio Take-off: Stock Market Theory.*

Other books by the author

Einstein in Verse: Introduction to Special and General Relativity

Life in Poetry: The Evolutionary "Garden of Eden"

IQ plus EQ: The Arrow and the Hoisting Crane

www.ingramcontent.com/pod-product-compliance
Lightning Source LLC
Chambersburg PA
CBHW071725170526
45165CB00005B/2163